Indiana FEVER

by Luke Hanlon

Copyright © 2026 by Press Room Editions. All rights reserved. No part of this book may be used or reproduced in any manner whatsoever, including internet usage, without written permission from the copyright owner, except in the case of brief quotations embodied in critical articles and reviews.

Book design by Kate Liestman
Cover design by Kate Liestman

Photographs ©: Tony Gutierrez/AP Images, cover; Cooper Neill/Getty Images Sport/Getty Images, 4, 7, 8; Otto Greule Jr./Allsport/Getty Images Sport/Getty Images, 10; John Harrell/AP Images, 13; Darron Cummings/AP Images, 15; Paul Battaglia/AP Images, 16; Christian Petersen/Getty Images Sport/Getty Images, 19; Pat Lovell/Cal Sport Media/AP Images, 21; Jeffrey Brown/Icon Sportswire/AP Images, 22; Andy Lyons/Getty Images Sport/Getty Images, 24, 29; Michael Hickey/Getty Images Sport/Getty Images, 26

Press Box Books, an imprint of Press Room Editions.

ISBN
979-8-89469-013-1 (library bound)
979-8-89469-026-1 (paperback)
979-8-89469-051-3 (epub)
979-8-89469-039-1 (hosted ebook)

Library of Congress Control Number: 2025930846

Distributed by North Star Editions, Inc.
2297 Waters Drive
Mendota Heights, MN 55120
www.northstareditions.com

Printed in the United States of America
082025

ABOUT THE AUTHOR

Luke Hanlon is a sportswriter and editor based in Minneapolis. He's written dozens of nonfiction sports books for kids and spends a lot of his free time watching his favorite Minnesota sports teams.

TABLE OF CONTENTS

CHAPTER 1
RECORD-BREAKING ROOKIE   5

CHAPTER 2
CATCHING A FEVER   11

CHAPTER 3
HEATING UP   17

CHAPTER 4
A NEW HOPE   23

SUPERSTAR PROFILE
TAMIKA CATCHINGS   28

QUICK STATS   30
GLOSSARY   31
TO LEARN MORE   32
INDEX   32

CHAPTER 1

RECORD-BREAKING ROOKIE

Caitlin Clark stormed down the court. The Indiana Fever point guard led a fast break. Clark dribbled hard toward the basket. A Dallas Wings defender stood in her way. So, Clark passed the ball behind her back. The ball bounced right to NaLyssa Smith. The forward scored easily, giving Clark an assist.

Caitlin Clark averaged 8.4 assists per game in 2024.

The Fever had taken Clark with the top pick in the 2024 Women's National Basketball Association (WNBA) Draft. Scouts raved about her shooting and passing skills. Now, Clark was putting on a passing clinic against Dallas. Her behind-the-back feed to Smith gave Clark 10 assists in the game. And more than five minutes still remained in the third quarter.

The Fever had trailed the Wings by 16 in the first half. But after Smith's bucket, Indiana trailed by only three. Clark's passing helped fuel the comeback. She continued to set up her teammates. By the end of the third quarter, she'd racked up 13 assists.

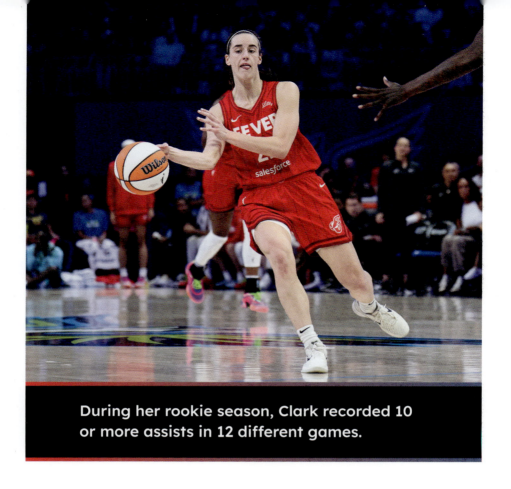

During her rookie season, Clark recorded 10 or more assists in 12 different games.

The Wings couldn't slow down Clark in the fourth quarter. With less than eight minutes to play, Clark dribbled into the paint. The defense collapsed toward her. Then Clark whipped a pass to the right corner. Lexie Hull buried the open three-pointer.

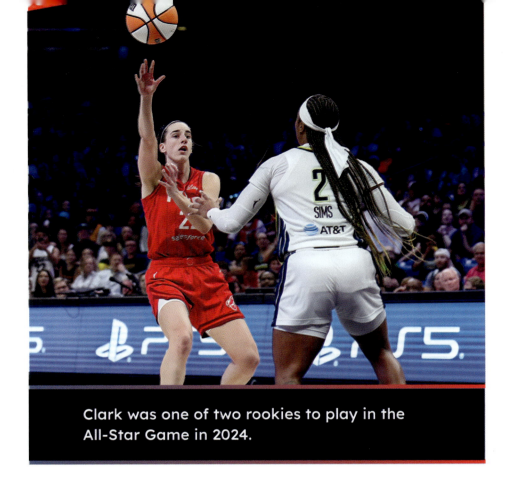

Clark was one of two rookies to play in the All-Star Game in 2024.

Minutes later, Clark lobbed a pass into the post. Aliyah Boston then scored easily off the feed. Clark now had 18 assists. That tied the WNBA record for most assists in a game.

Two possessions later, Clark had the ball again. The Fever trailed by three. Two defenders trapped Clark in the paint. She quickly lofted the ball back outside the arc. Kelsey Mitchell stood alone behind the three-point line. Her shot rattled in to tie the game. It also secured Clark's 19th assist.

HISTORIC SEASON

Caitlin Clark enjoyed one of the best rookie seasons in WNBA history. She finished 2024 with 337 assists. That broke the league record for most assists in a season. Clark also averaged 19.2 points per game. She earned a spot on the All-WNBA First Team. Clark became the first rookie to make that team since 2008.

The Wings ended up winning 101–93. But Clark's record-breaking performance against Dallas was one of many highlights during her rookie year. Fever fans couldn't wait to see what she would do next.

CHAPTER 2

CATCHING A FEVER

The Indiana Fever joined the WNBA in 2000. They were one of four expansion teams that year. The Fever built their roster mostly with bench players from other teams. Without top talent, Indiana won only nine games in 2000.

The Fever's poor record helped them get the third pick in the 2001 draft.

Rita Williams played in the All-Star Game with Indiana in 2001.

They used that pick on Tamika Catchings. The University of Tennessee forward had been the best player in women's college basketball in 2000. Then she suffered a knee injury during her senior year. Teams knew Catchings couldn't play at all in 2001. But the Fever drafted her anyway. That's how confident Indiana was that Catchings would be a star.

Catchings proved to be worth the wait. She made her debut in the first game of the 2002 season. In a

> **MAKING THE TEAM**
>
> The Fever held open tryouts before their first season. More than 200 players showed up. Only one of them made the team, though. Texlin Quinney played in 17 games for the Fever in 2000. She recorded three assists in Indiana's first-ever win.

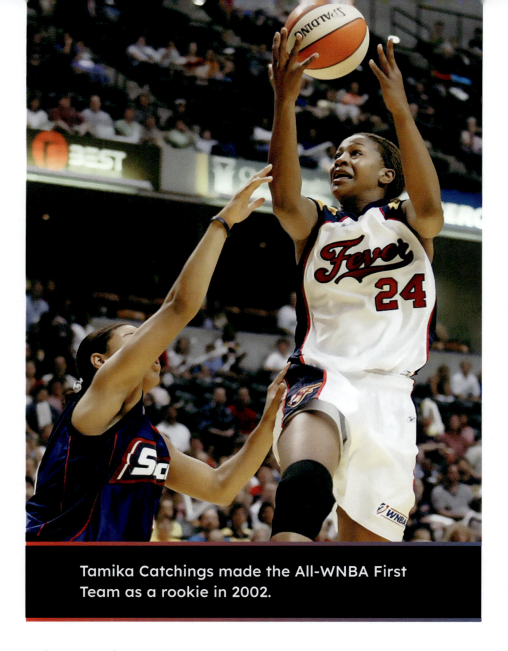

Tamika Catchings made the All-WNBA First Team as a rookie in 2002.

win against the Detroit Shock, Catchings recorded 23 points, 13 rebounds, and 5 steals. She went on to win Rookie of the Year honors. More importantly, she lifted the Fever to their first playoff appearance. However, the New York Liberty beat Indiana in the first round.

Catchings continued to lead the Fever for years. Her tough defense rubbed off on her teammates. By 2005, the Fever had one of the best defenses in the WNBA. They made it back to the playoffs that year. Once again, Indiana faced the Liberty in the first round. This time, the Fever swept New York.

The Fever faced the Connecticut Sun in the semifinals. The Sun won Game 1 in Indiana. A loss in Game 2 would end the Fever's season. Down 60–57, Catchings nailed a three-pointer with 18 seconds

Catchings averaged more than two steals per game in her career.

to go. That shot sent the game to overtime. Unfortunately for Indiana fans, the Sun closed out the series with a 77–67 win.

CHAPTER 3

HEATING UP

Tamika Catchings started 2007 on a tear. But she injured her foot midway through the season. Anna DeForge stepped up without her. The All-Star guard helped the Fever reach the playoffs.

Catchings returned to face Connecticut in the first round. The Sun won Game 1 in triple overtime.

Anna DeForge made 41 percent of her three-pointers in 2007.

But DeForge poured in 26 points in Game 2 to tie the series. Then Catchings took over in Game 3. She recorded 30 points and 13 rebounds to bring Indiana to the semifinals.

The Detroit Shock had ended Indiana's season in 2006. In the 2007 semifinals, the teams met in a decisive Game 3. The Fever jumped out to an early lead. However, Catchings suffered an injury just before halftime. Without their star, the Fever lost to the Shock again.

Before the 2008 season, the Fever traded for Katie Douglas. The All-Star guard had grown up in Indianapolis. Douglas thrived playing for her hometown team. But she couldn't lift the Fever to a

Katie Douglas played in the All-Star Game twice with the Fever.

series win over Detroit. Indiana fell to the Shock in the first round.

The rivals met again in the 2009 semifinals. This time, Catchings was fully healthy. She helped the Fever take down the Shock in three games. For the first time, Indiana was headed to the WNBA Finals.

The Fever and the Phoenix Mercury split the first two games of the series. In Game 3, Ebony Hoffman put Indiana up one with a late jump shot. The Fever hung on to win 86–85. But the Mercury won the next two games to claim the title.

OUTDOOR BASKETBALL

The Indiana Fever made history in 2008. That year, they played against the New York Liberty at Arthur Ashe Stadium. That venue is an outdoor tennis stadium in New York. The matchup marked the first regular-season professional basketball game held outdoors. The Fever beat the Liberty 71–55.

Shavonte Zellous celebrates winning the 2012 WNBA Finals.

The Fever returned to the Finals in 2012. They faced the defending champion Minnesota Lynx. The Fever weren't fazed, though. The Lynx struggled to stop Catchings. And Shavonte Zellous provided scoring throughout the series. Together, they led the Fever to their first title.

CHAPTER 4

A NEW HOPE

Indiana didn't slow down after winning the championship in 2012. The Fever made it back to the semifinals in 2013 and 2014. However, they lost each time. A year later, Tamika Catchings led them on another deep playoff run.

The Fever faced the Chicago Sky in the first round. The teams played a

Catchings played in the All-Star Game 10 times during her career.

Briann January averaged 3.6 assists per game during her nine seasons with Indiana.

decisive Game 3 in Chicago. Catchings scored 27 points to win the series. In the semifinals, the Fever traveled to New York for Game 3. Indiana guard Briann January racked up eight assists and six steals against the Liberty. She helped the Fever return to the Finals.

Indiana stayed hot on the road. The Fever won Game 1 in Minnesota. But the Lynx battled back. The series went to a Game 5. This time, the Lynx protected their home court to win the title.

Catchings played her final WNBA season in 2016. At 37 years old, she led the Fever to the playoffs for the 12th straight year. However, they lost in the first round.

The Fever missed Catchings after she retired. Starting in 2017, Indiana suffered six straight losing seasons. In 2022, the team won only five games. That tough season came with some good

Aliyah Boston averaged 8.4 rebounds per game in 2023.

news, though. The Fever received the top pick in the 2023 draft. They selected Aliyah Boston. The forward could take over games in the paint. Boston won the Rookie of the Year Award. Even so, Indiana still finished with one of the league's worst records.

Excitement in Indiana couldn't have been higher for the 2024 season. Fever fans regularly sold out their arena to watch Caitlin Clark, the year's top draft pick. The team got off to a slow start, though. The Fever lost eight of their first nine games. Then Clark led a turnaround. Behind the Rookie of the Year, the Fever made the playoffs. Even though Indiana lost in the first round, Clark and Boston gave fans plenty of hope for the future.

FAMILIAR FACE

Stephanie White played for the Fever from 2000 to 2004. In 2011, the team hired her to be an assistant coach. White took over as Indiana's head coach in 2015. She left the Fever after two seasons. But the team hired her again. White returned as Indiana's head coach in 2025.

SUPERSTAR PROFILE

TAMIKA CATCHINGS

Tamika Catchings could do it all. On offense, she scored in the paint. She drained three-pointers, too. Catchings also grabbed loads of rebounds.

Catchings's greatest skill may have been her effort. She hustled for loose balls. And she never seemed to get tired. Those traits allowed her to dominate on defense. Catchings could shut down an opposing team's best scorer. She regularly forced turnovers, too. Catchings finished her career with a WNBA record 1,074 steals. She also won Defensive Player of the Year honors a record five times.

Catchings's top moment with Indiana came in the 2012 Finals. She averaged 22.3 points and 6 rebounds per game in that series. That performance helped her earn the Finals Most Valuable Player (MVP) Award.

Catchings was voted into the Basketball Hall of Fame in 2020.

QUICK STATS

INDIANA FEVER

Founded: 2000

Championships: 1 (2012)

Key coaches:
- Brian Winters (2004–07): 78–58, 5–7 playoffs
- Lin Dunn (2008–14): 135–103, 23–18 playoffs, 1 WNBA title
- Stephanie White (2015–16, 2025–): 37–31, 6–6 playoffs

Most career points: Tamika Catchings (7,380)

Most career assists: Tamika Catchings (1,488)

Most career rebounds: Tamika Catchings (3,315)

Most career blocks: Tamika Catchings (385)

Most career steals: Tamika Catchings (1,074)

Stats are accurate through the 2024 season.

GLOSSARY

debut
First appearance.

draft
An event that allows teams to choose new players coming into the league.

expansion teams
New teams that are added to an existing league.

fast break
A play in which a team moves the ball up the floor quickly.

paint
The area between the basket and the free-throw line.

rivals
Opposing players or teams that bring out the greatest emotion from fans and players.

rookie
A first-year player.

roster
A list of players on a team.

scouts
People who look for talented young players.

swept
Won all the games in a series.

TO LEARN MORE

Anderson, Josh. *Indiana Fever*. Lerner Publications, 2025.
Hewson, Anthony K. *Caitlin Clark*. Press Box Books, 2024.
O'Neal, Ciara. *The WNBA Finals*. Apex Editions, 2023.

MORE INFORMATION

To learn more about the Indiana Fever, go to **pressboxbooks.com/AllAccess**. These links are routinely monitored and updated to provide the most current information available.

INDEX

Boston, Aliyah, 8, 26–27

Catchings, Tamika, 12–14, 17–21, 23–25, 28
Chicago Sky, 23–24
Clark, Caitlin, 5–9, 27
Connecticut Sun, 14–15, 17

Dallas Wings, 5–7, 9
DeForge, Anna, 17–18
Detroit Shock, 13, 18–20
Douglas, Katie, 18

Hoffman, Ebony, 20
Hull, Lexie, 7

January, Briann, 24–25

Minnesota Lynx, 21, 25
Mitchell, Kelsey, 9

New York Liberty, 14, 20, 24–25

Phoenix Mercury, 20

Quinney, Texlin, 12

Smith, NaLyssa, 5–6

White, Stephanie, 27

Zellous, Shavonte, 21